NEIGHBOURS
and other
TV Themes

Edited by PETER FOSS
Arranged by GARY LERNER

Cover design by Graphic Edge
Photographs by Eirik Hevroy Berg
Richmond College

First Published 1989
© International Music Publications

Exclusive Distributors
International Music Publications
Southend Road, Woodford Green,
Essex IG8 8HN, England.

Yvonne Dunn
Innercraigie Farm
Madderty
Porthotuire
PH7 8NY

£4.50

215-2-543

FINGERING CHART

Recorder

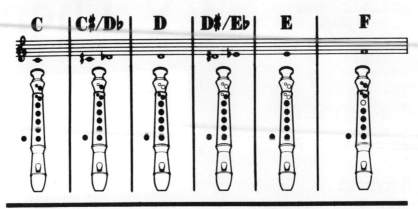

CHORD DIRECTORY

Guitar

'x' over a string means this string should not be played

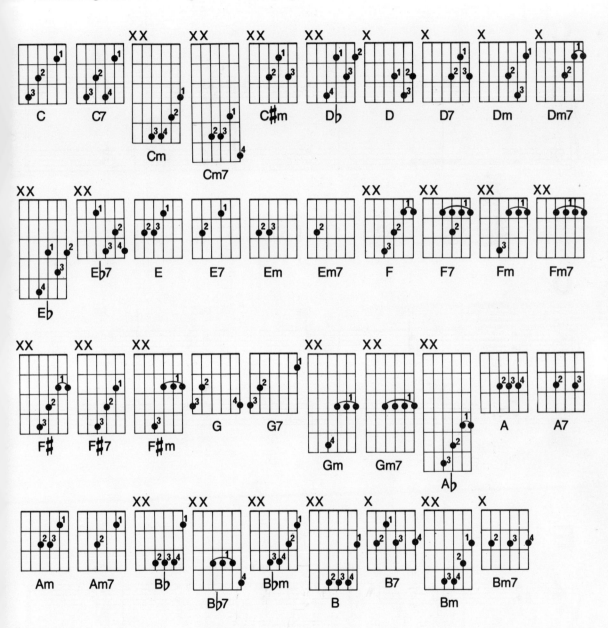

Always make sure your guitar is in tune with the other instruments before you start to play with other musicians.

CHORD SYMBOL GUIDE

Keyboards

C

D

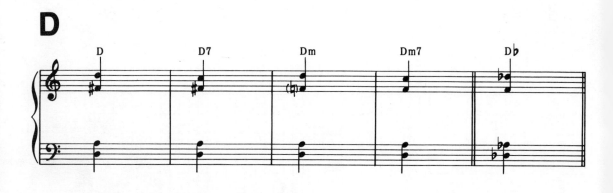

E

F

G

A

B

'ALLO 'ALLO

By DAVID CROFT
and ROY MOORE

EASTENDERS

By LESLIE OSBORNE
and SIMON MAY

CORONATION STREET

By ERIC SPEAR

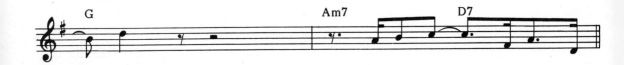

ritard.

FAME

Words by DEAN PITCHFORD
Music by MICHAEL GORE

Moderately fast, with a driving beat

Ba-by, look at me, ——— and tell me

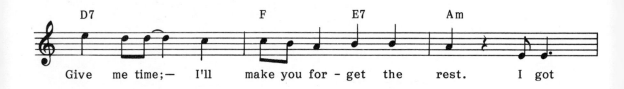

what you see. — You ain't seen — the best — of me yet.

Give me time; — I'll make you for - get the rest. I got

more in me, ——— and you can set it free. —

I can catch — the moon — in my hand. Don't you know — who I

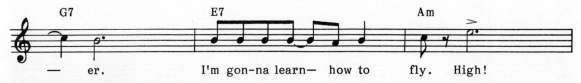

am? Re-mem-ber my name. Fame! I'm gon-na live — for ev —

— er. I'm gon-na learn — how to fly. High!

FAWLTY TOWERS

By DENNIS WILSON

HEAVEN

By DAVID ROSE

HILL STREET BLUES

By MIKE POST

ritard.

I WISH I KNEW HOW IT WOULD FEEL TO BE FREE
(Film 89)

Words by BILLY TAYLOR and DICK DALLAS
Music by BILLY TAYLOR

I COULD BE SO GOOD FOR YOU

Words and Music by
PATRICIA WATERMAN and GERARD KENNY

Moderately, strong beat

There ain't nothing I can't go through, —————— I'd be so good— for you.

[1] you. Don't ask— me no ques-tions, I'll tell— you no lies.

[2] you. Don't ask— me no ques-tions, I'll tell— you no lies.

Use my shoulder to rest — on, I will be right by your side, I will be your ear to-night. I could be so good for you,—

Love you like you want me to,— I can ev — en help you breathe,———————— I'd be so good— for you.

LOVE IS LIKE A BUTTERFLY

Words and Music
by DOLLY PARTON

Moderately bright

Love is like a but-ter-fly, as soft and gen-tle

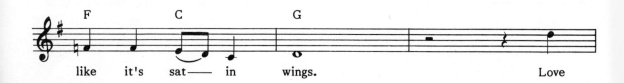

as a sigh. The mul-ti-col-oured moods— of love are

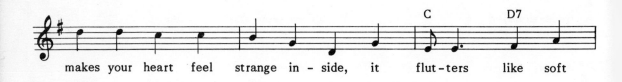

like it's sat— in wings. Love

makes your heart feel strange in-side, it flut-ters like soft

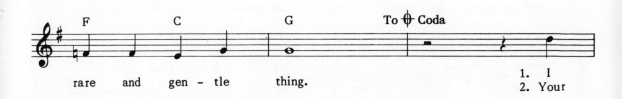

wings in flight. Love is like— a but-ter-fly, a

rare and gen-tle thing. 1. I
2. Your

feel it when you're with me, it hap-pens when you
laugh-ter brings me sun-shine, ev-'ry day is

LAST OF THE SUMMER WINE

By RONNIE HAZLEHURST

(Meg's Bong)

MISS MARPLE

By K
and ALA

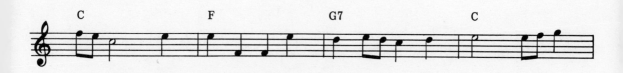

THEME FROM M.A.S.H.

Words by MIKE ALTMAN
Music by JOHNNY MANDEL

MATCH OF THE DAY

By RHET STOLLER

NEIGHBOURS

Words and Music by
TONY HATCH and JACKIE TRENT

Swing rhythm

Neigh——bours, ev-'ry-bo-dy needs good

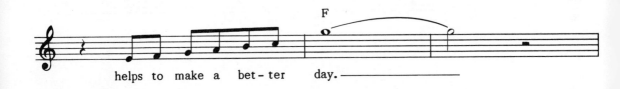

neigh——bours, just a friend-ly wave each morn——ing

helps to make a bet-ter day.——

Neigh——bours need to get to know each

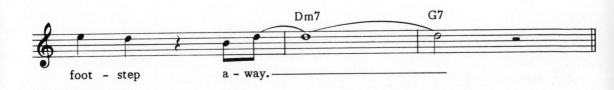

oth——er, next door is on——ly a

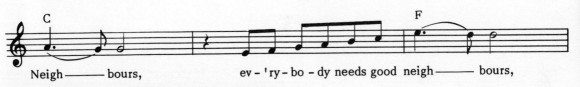

foot-step a-way.——

Neigh——bours, ev-'ry-bo-dy needs good neigh——bours,

ONE MOMENT IN TIME

Words and Music by
ALBERT HAMMOND and JOHN BETTIS

THANK YOU FOR BEING A FRIEND

Words and Music
by ANDREW GOLD

Moderately fast

Thank-you for be - ing a friend,——

Trav - elled down the road and back a - gain.—— Your

heart is true— you're a pal and a con - fi - dant.——

I'm not a-shamed— to say ——

I hope it al - ways will stay —— this way.— My

hat is off— won't you stand up and take a bow? —

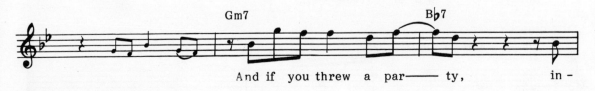

And if you threw a par——ty, in-

vit-ed ev-'ry-one you knew,—— You would see—— the big-gest

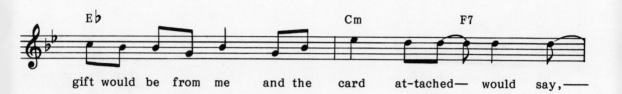

gift would be from me and the card at-tached—— would say,——

—— Thank-you for be - ing a friend,——

Thank-you for be - ing a friend,——

Thank-you for be-ing a friend,——

Thank-you for be-ing a friend.——

THAT'S LIVING ALRIGHT

Words and Music by
DAVID MACKAY and KEN ASHBY

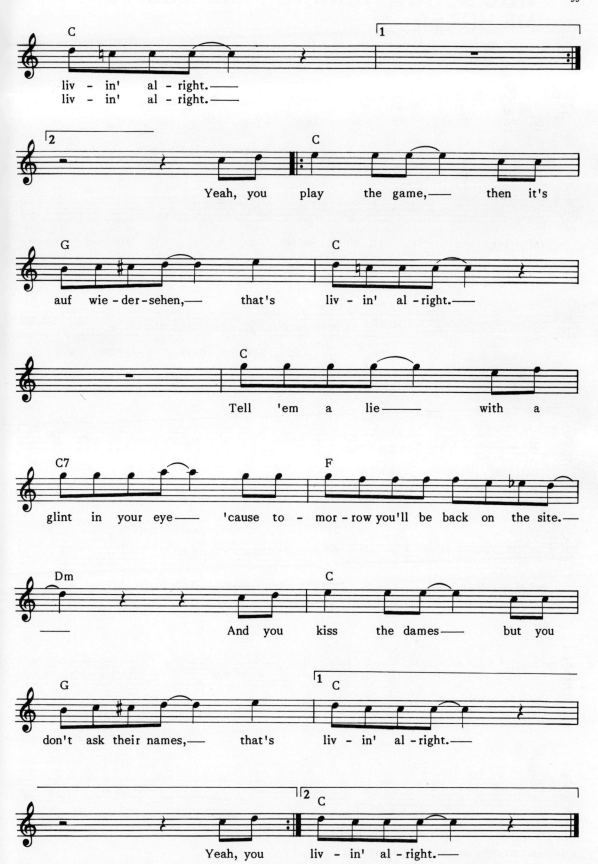

liv - in' al - right.——
liv - in' al - right.——

Yeah, you play the game,—— then it's

auf wie - der - sehen,—— that's liv - in' al - right.——

Tell 'em a lie—— with a

glint in your eye—— 'cause to - mor - row you'll be back on the site.——

—— And you kiss the dames—— but you

don't ask their names,—— that's liv - in' al - right.——

Yeah, you liv - in' al - right.——

WHO DO YOU THINK YOU ARE KIDDING, MR HITLER

Words by JIMMY PERRY
Music by JIMMY PERRY and DEREK TAVERNER

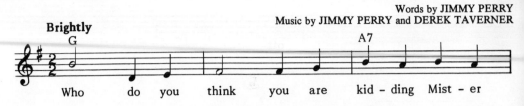

Who do you think you are kid - ding Mist - er

Hit - ler, If you think we're on the run?

We are the boys who will

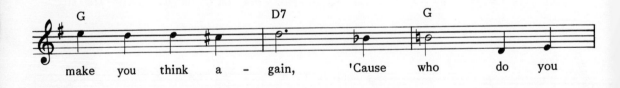

stop your lit - tle game, We are the boys who will

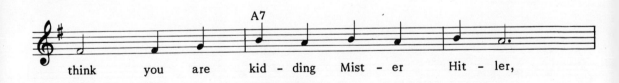

make you think a - gain, 'Cause who do you

think you are kid - ding Mist - er Hit - ler,

If you think old Eng - land's done?

STAR TREK

Words by GENE RODDENBERRY
Music by ALEXANDER COURAGE

Fast rhythmic beat

Be - yond the rim of the star - light My love is wan-d'ring in star flight. I know he'll find in star-clus-tered reach - es, Love strange love a star-wo-man teach - es. I know his jour-ney ends nev - er. His star trek will go on for - ev - er, But tell him while he wan-ders his star - ry sea Re - mem - ber, re-mem-ber me. me.

Printed in England by Callgraving Limited Thetford Norfolk